# Endangered Wolves

## Bobbie Kalman

Crabtree Publishing Company

www.crabtreebooks.com

# Earth's Endangered Animals Series
## A Bobbie Kalman Book
Dedicated by Katherine Kantor
To my sweetheart Matt—I love you

**Author and Editor-in-Chief**
Bobbie Kalman

**Substantive editor**
Kelley MacAulay

**Research**
Laura Hysert

**Editors**
Molly Aloian
Amanda Bishop
Kristina Lundblad
Kathryn Smithyman

**Art director**
Robert MacGregor

**Design**
Katherine Kantor

**Production coordinator**
Katherine Kantor

**Photo research**
Crystal Foxton

**Consultant**
Patricia Loesche, Ph.D., Animal Behavior Program,
Department of Psychology, University of Washington

**Photographs**
© Charlie Hamilton James/naturepl.com: page 15
All other images by Corbis, Corel, Creatas, and
Digital Stock

**Illustrations**
Barbara Bedell: border, pages 4, 7 (red wolf), 13
Katherine Kantor: page 14
Margaret Amy Reiach: back cover, pages 5,
    7 (Ethiopian wolf, gray wolf), 16

## Crabtree Publishing Company
www.crabtreebooks.com          1-800-387-7650

Cataloging-in-Publication Data
Kalman, Bobbie.
  Endangered wolves / Bobbie Kalman.
    p. cm. -- (Earth's endangered animals series)
Includes index.
  ISBN 0-7787-1854-9 (RLB) -- ISBN 0-7787-1900-6 (pbk.)
  1. Wolves--Juvenile literature. 2. Endangered species--Juvenile
literature. I. Title.
  QL737.C22K355 2004
  599.773--dc22
                                                    2004014156
                                                    LC

**Published in
the United States**
PMB16A
350 Fifth Ave.
Suite 3308
New York, NY
10118

**Published
in Canada**
616 Welland Ave.,
St. Catharines, Ontario
Canada
L2M 5V6

**Published in the
United Kingdom**
73 Lime Walk
Headington
Oxford
OX3 7AD
United Kingdom

**Published
in Australia**
386 Mt. Alexander Rd.,
Ascot Vale (Melbourne)
VIC 3032

# Contents

# Endangered!

In the past, there were as many as two million wolves. There are now fewer than 200,000! Most wolves are **vulnerable**, but a few types are **critically endangered**. Endangered animals are at risk of disappearing from the Earth forever. If they are not protected, they may become **extinct**. Extinct animals are gone from the Earth.

## Words to know

Scientists use special words to talk about animals that are in danger. Some of these words are listed below.

**vulnerable** Describes animals that may soon become endangered

**endangered** Describes animals that are in danger of dying out in the natural places where they live

**critically endangered** Describes animals that are at high risk of dying out in the **wild**, or places that are not controlled by people

**extinct** Describes animals that have died out or that have not been seen alive in the wild for at least 50 years

# What are wolves?

Wolves belong to a group of animals called **mammals**. Mammals are **warm-blooded**. The bodies of warm-blooded animals stay about the same temperature, no matter how hot or cold their surroundings are. Mammals have backbones, and some have hair or fur on their bodies. Baby mammals **nurse**, or drink milk from their mothers' bodies.

## Canids

Wolves are the largest **canids**, or members of the *Canidae* family. This family also includes coyotes, jackals, foxes, and **domestic**, or pet, dogs. Canids are **carnivores**, or meat-eaters. All canids have long **snouts**. They also have separate toes and sharp claws.

# Three types of wolves

There are three main types of wolves—red wolves, Ethiopian wolves, and gray wolves. There are many **subgroups**, or kinds, of gray wolves.

## Red wolves

Red wolves are critically endangered. Scientists believe there are fewer than 300 red wolves left in the world. Of the 300 red wolves alive, only about 100 live in the wild. The remaining wolves live in **captivity**.

## Ethiopian wolves

Ethiopian wolves are critically endangered. Scientists believe that there are fewer than 550 Ethiopian wolves left on Earth. Ethiopian wolves are also known as Abyssinian wolves.

## Gray wolves

Gray wolves are vulnerable. Many subgroups of gray wolves are endangered, however. There are fewer than 200,000 gray wolves on Earth.

## How many types?

Scientists often disagree about how many types of wolves there are. Some scientists believe that gray wolves, red wolves, and Ethiopian wolves are three different types of wolves. Others believe that all wolves are gray wolves and that red wolves and Ethiopian wolves are two more subgroups of gray wolves.

# Wolf packs

Wolves live in **packs**, or groups of several family members. Most packs are made up of four to seven wolves. Only two wolves in a pack **mate**, or join together to make babies. All the other wolves in the pack are the **offspring**, or children, of the two mating wolves. As the offspring get older, they leave their parents' pack to form new packs of their own.

*The wolves in a pack protect and care for one another. They show affection by touching their noses, wagging their tails, and holding their bodies close together.*

## Leaders of the pack

The **parent wolves** are usually the two strongest members of a wolf pack. If one parent gets hurt or dies, another strong wolf takes its place. The male parent is in charge of the pack's hunting activities.

## The first to eat

After a successful hunt, the parent wolves are the first two wolves to eat. The offspring must wait until the parent wolves are finished eating. The offspring then eat whatever meat is left.

# Where do wolves live?

A **habitat** is the natural place where an animal lives. Gray wolves live in many habitats, such as forests, grasslands, and the **tundra**. Gray wolf habitats are found mainly in Canada, Russia, and Mongolia. Red wolves live in grassland and forest habitats. They live only in North Carolina, in the United States. Ethiopian wolves live only in the **mountainous** habitats of Ethiopia, a country in Africa.

*Arctic wolves are a subgroup of gray wolves. They are named after the Arctic, the northern place where they live.*

## Wolf territories

Each wolf pack has its own **territory**, or area of land within a habitat. The parent wolves hunt for food and raise their offspring in their territory. They mark the **boundaries**, or edges, of their territory by scratching the ground and the bark of trees.

## Leaving their scents

Another way wolves mark their territories is by leaving behind their **scents**, or smells. They leave their scents mainly by **urinating**. When other wolves smell the urine, they stay off the territory to avoid fighting with the pack that hunts there.

*Wolf territories can be large or small. Wolves that live in areas with cold winters, such as the wolf shown above, have large territories because food is harder to find in cold weather. Wolves that live in warmer places have smaller territories because food is easier to find all year.*

# A wolf's body

Wolves have fur coats. Gray wolves usually live in places that are cold for part of the year, so they have thick coats to keep them warm. The coats of gray wolves can be many colors, from shades of gray and brown to pure white or black.

Red wolves and Ethiopian wolves have thinner coats than those of gray wolves because these wolves live in areas where the weather is usually warm. The coats of red wolves and Ethiopian wolves are reddish brown in color.

*Ethiopian wolves and red wolves, such as the red wolf shown above, are smaller in size than are gray wolves.*

# Built for hunting

Wolves have strong, muscular bodies that are perfect for catching **prey**. They use their long legs to run quickly through mud and snow. Wolves also have large feet that help them travel over rocks and uneven ground.

*Wolves have very good hearing. Their large ears help them hear sounds from far away.*

*Wolves have long, bushy tails. They use their tails to show certain emotions. For example, when wolves are scared, they pull their tails between their legs, just as dogs do.*

*Wolves use their sharp teeth to catch and eat prey. They use their powerful jaws to hold their prey.*

13

# Wolf food

Wolves are **predators**. They spend many hours a day hunting for prey animals. A pack of wolves usually hunts large animals such as deer and moose. Wolves also eat rabbits, **rodents**, beavers, and birds. When prey is scarce, wolves will eat insects, nuts, berries, and fruits. When there is plenty to eat, wolves bury some food in **caches**, or hidden places, to prepare for times when food is difficult to find.

*A wolf usually eats five to twelve pounds (2.3 to 5.4 kg) of meat per day.*

## On the hunt

Living in packs helps wolves hunt for food. The wolves in a pack are able to chase down and capture more prey when they work as a team. They use their keen senses of hearing and smell to find a **herd**, or group, of prey, such as deer or caribou. They chase the herd and attack the slowest or weakest animal. It is difficult for a pack to catch the animal, however. If a chase lasts too long, the wolves give up.

*Although Ethiopian wolves live in packs, they often hunt alone. Each wolf catches small prey, such as a mouse, by stabbing it with its front legs.*

# A wolf's life cycle

Every animal goes through a set of changes called a **life cycle**. A life cycle is made up of all the changes that happen to an animal from the time it is born to the time it becomes **mature**. A mature animal can mate and have babies of its own. With each baby, a new life cycle begins.

## A gray wolf's life cycle

*A gray wolf begins its life cycle inside its mother's body. The **pup**, or baby wolf, is born in a **litter**, or group of pups. Each litter has four to seven pups.*

*Gray wolves mature between two and four years of age.*

*When a wolf is about six months old, it is called a **juvenile**. Juveniles spend a lot of time playing together! They jump on one another and wrestle.*

*The pup nurses for at least four weeks. It then starts eating other foods as well.*

16

## Growing up

When a female wolf is ready to give birth, she finds a **den**. A den is a safe shelter where she gives birth and takes care of her pups after they are born. The pups live in the den for the first three to four weeks of their lives. The pack protects the den from predators.

## Outside the den

When the pups are one to two months old, they join the rest of the pack at a **rendezvous site**, or meeting place. The pups grow, play, and learn to hunt at the rendezvous site. When the pups become juveniles, they learn to hunt with the pack.

*This mother wolf is carefully protecting her young pups from danger.*

# Wolf behavior

Wolves **communicate**, or send messages to one another, using body positions and facial expressions. Parent wolves show that they are in charge by standing tall with their tails held up in the air. The offspring in the pack hold their bodies close to the ground, with their tails hanging low. Some wolves, such as the one shown above, may even lie on the ground. Wolves wag their tails when they are happy or when they want to play. When wolves are angry, they show their teeth and growl.

## Howls and growls

Wolves also communicate with one another by making sounds, such as barks, growls, whines, snarls, and howls. Howls are the most famous wolf sounds.

Wolves howl for many reasons. They often howl as a group before going on a hunt. Wolves also howl to locate a lost pup. The wolves in a pack can recognize one another's voices.

# Habitat loss

The biggest threat to wolves is **habitat loss**. Habitat loss means losing the natural areas of land in which animals live and find food. Each year there are more people on Earth, and they need land for building homes and growing food. People **clear**, or remove plants from, large areas of wolf habitats to make space for cities and farmland.

## Losing their food

When land is cleared, the animals that wolves hunt cannot find enough food to eat. Many of these animals starve to death. Soon, many wolves have trouble finding food, and they starve as well.

*When people and wolves live close together, wolves often catch diseases from pet dogs.*

## Searching for a meal

As wild prey become hard to find, wolves must find other food to eat. Some wolves go to farms and eat **livestock**, or animals that people raise for food, such as cattle and sheep. In the past, farmers killed thousands of wolves every year to protect their livestock. In many areas, farmers killed so many wolves that the animals became extinct in those areas. Today, it is **illegal**, or against the law, to kill wolves in some countries, but many people continue to break this law.

*Wolf packs actually kill very few livestock. Each year, more cows and sheep die from diseases, bad weather, and dog attacks than they do from wolf attacks.*

# Hunting wolves

Some people get angry when wolves kill livestock and animals, such as deer and moose, that people want to hunt. Others are frightened of wolves. In the past, many people wanted all wolves to be destroyed.

## Bounty hunters

In the 1800s, governments in the United States, Canada, and parts of western Europe offered people **bounties**, or rewards of money, to kill wolves. By 1900, nearly all the wolves in the United States and western Europe had been hunted for bounties. The bounty hunting that took place in the past is the main reason that wolves are endangered today.

*For many years, people believed that wolves attacked human beings. Wolves almost always run away from people, however.*

## The hunting continues

Today, fewer people are frightened of wolves. Wolves are still hunted for sport and by farmers around the world, however. In Canada and Alaska, hunting wolves is legal. There are also very few limits on hunting wolves in much of Eastern Europe, Asia, and the Middle East. Some hunters use traps that have sharp spikes. These traps cause wolves a lot of pain! Hunters are supposed to check their traps every day, but few do. Every year, thousands of wolves die in these traps.

### No pet wolves!

Some people believe that they are helping wolves by keeping them as pets, but wolves are not pets! They belong in the wild. When they are kept as pets, wolves do not have enough space or proper food to eat. Although they rarely attack people, wolves may attack their owners if they feel threatened. Wolves cannot be trained to forget their natural behaviors!

23

# Back into the wild

Many people realize that wolves play an important role in nature. Some scientists believe that wolves should be **reintroduced** to the wild places where they once lived.

To reintroduce wolves means to take wolves raised in captivity to wild areas and release them. When wolves are reintroduced into the wild, people no longer feed and look after them.

*When wolves are reintroduced into an area, the relationships among animals—and even plants—change. Wolves hunt some large animals, such as deer and elk. The remains of these animals feed other animals in winter. The rest of the remains makes the soil a healthier place for new plants to grow.*

## Saving red wolves

Red wolves once lived throughout the southeastern United States. **Over-hunting** and habitat loss have caused red wolves to become almost extinct. To save red wolves, the United States Fish and Wildlife Service captured some of the wolves from the wild. In captivity, the wolves mated and had pups. Scientists helped keep the pups alive, and soon the number of red wolves began to grow. In 1987, the United States Fish and Wildlife Service began reintroducing the captive red wolves to the wild in North Carolina. Today, there are more than 100 red wolves living in the wild.

## Not enough land

Reintroduced wolves can face many problems. When they are reintroduced to the wild, they are given only small areas of land as their territories. As the wolves mate and have pups, however, they need larger territories in which to hunt. To find food, wolves sometimes hunt on lands that are outside their territories.

## Afraid of wolves

Many people who live near the territories of reintroduced wolves feel the wolves are **pests**. Some farmers believe the wolves will kill their livestock. Other people think wolves hunt too many of the same animals that people hunt. Reintroduced wolves are often hunted illegally by people who do not want wolves in their area.

*Wolves are important because they hunt the sick, old, or very young animals in a herd. When some of these animals are gone, there is more food for the healthy herd animals.*

# Safe wild places

Wolves need safe wild places in which to live. Some countries are helping wolves by creating **national parks** and **preserves**. National parks are areas of land set aside by a country's government to protect the plants and animals that live on the land. Preserves protect one or more types of animals. Wolf packs that live in national parks and preserves are safe to roam and search for food.

## Protecting the wolves

Park and preserve **rangers** are workers who protect the animals that live in national parks and preserves. They keep track of the wolves and their territories, and they help sick or injured animals.

Park and preserve rangers also protect wild animals from hunters. They stop hunters from shooting animals and remove the traps the hunters have set.

*Wolf preserves are closed to the public in late winter and early spring. During these times, wolves mate and give birth to pups.*

# Wolves in zoos

Today, many people are working hard to protect wolves! Endangered wolves often find safe homes in zoos. Scientists and zookeepers try to increase the **population**, or total number, of wolves.

Many zoos have **captive breeding plans**. These plans give wolves safe places to mate and raise their young. With each new pup, the zoos are saving critically endangered wolves from becoming extinct.

*The best zoos have teams of scientists who study and care for the captive wolves.*

29

# Wonderful wolves

The more you learn about wolves, the more you will want to help them! There are many ways you can get involved in the fight to save endangered wolves.

## Making a difference

Ask your friends to help you raise some money at an event, such as a bake sale or a car wash. Then donate the money to your favorite wolf organization. You and your family can also adopt a wolf from an organization such as Wolf Haven International (see page 31). By adopting a wolf, you will ensure that one wolf has proper food and shelter.

*Every summer, people gather in wolf preserves to hear wolf packs howl. If you live near a preserve, try to attend a wolf howl. Hearing wolves howl will make you want to know more about these amazing animals.*

## Wolves on the web

Learn more about wolves and how you can help them by clicking on these great Internet sites:

• **www.kidsplanet.org/www/**
At World Wide Wolves, you'll learn about different types of wolves and test your wolf smarts!

• **www.wolf.org/wolves/learn/learn.asp**
The International Wolf Center lets you watch wolves live on video! To see the wolves, click on "Experience" and then "Watch wolves cam."

• **www.wolfhaven.org**
Get to know the wolves living at Wolf Haven International through pictures, stories, and video clips.

# Glossary

Note: Boldfaced words that are defined in the text may not appear in the glossary.

**captivity** A state of being in an enclosed area such as a zoo

**carnivore** An animal that eats other animals

**domestic** Animals that are raised by humans to be pets

**mountainous** An area of land with many mountains

**over-hunting** Hunting too many animals and causing them to become endangered or extinct

**predator** An animal that hunts and kills other animals for food

**prey** An animal that is eaten by other animals

**pest** An animal that is considered troublesome to humans

**rodent** A small animal that has front teeth that never stop growing

**snout** The front part of a wolf's head

**tundra** A treeless area in an arctic region

**urinate** To release waste fluid from the body

**vulnerable** Describes animals that may soon become endangered

# Index

1 2 3 4 5 6 7 8 9 0   Printed in the U.S.A.   4 3 2 1 0 9 8 7 6 5